Platform

PLATFORM

14 Steps

To a Brand new you

Dawn Ferguson

TiesBowtiesLipstick,LLC

Copyright © 2014 by TiesBowtiesLipstick, LLC

All rights reserved. No part of this publication may be reproduced, distributed, or transmitted in any form or by any means, including photocopying, recording, or other electronic or mechanical methods, without the prior written permission of the publisher, except in the case of brief quotations embodied in critical reviews and certain other noncommercial uses permitted by copyright law. For permission requests, write to the publisher, addressed "Attention: Permissions Coordinator," at the address below.

TiesBowtiesLipstick, LLC

1134 So Black Horse Pike #242

Blackwood, NJ 08012

www.tiesbowtieslipstick.com

ISBN-10: 0990958108
ISBN-13: 978-0-9909581-0-9

Ordering Autographed Copies or Seminar Information:

www.tiesbowtieslipstick.com.

Printed in the United States of America

Dedication

To

My Family & Friends

For all of my family and friends who have shaped me into the person I am today. Most of all to my parents you rock and I appreciate all you've done for me. To my husband and children thank you for putting up with me. Last but not least thank you for letting me be me.

Love, Dawn (Mz Originator)

Table of Contents:

Part I. **Too Much to Carry**

Chapter 1. *Clearing Your Mind* 3

Chapter 2. *Change the Way You Think* 11

Chapter 3. *Get Out of Your Own Way* 19

Part II **What Lies Underneath**

Chapter 4. *If I Die Today* 31

Chapter 5. *Look For Motivation* 37

Chapter 6. *Learn From Your Failures* 41

Chapter 7. *Outgrowing Friends Is a Process of Growth* 49

Chapter 8. *Don't Be Afraid to Close Doors* 55

Part III **Bringing Fourth Your Platform**

Chapter 9. *Kissing the Old You Goodbye* **65**

Chapter 10. *Embracing the New You* **71**

Chapter 11. *Turn Your Fears into Accomplishments* **77**

Chapter 12. *Put Your Plans into Action* **83**

Chapter 13. *Jump Take a Chance* **89**

Chapter 14. *Don't Settle* **95**

Introduction

Platform is the book that helps you rediscover your true and inner qualities. It helps you to bring forth the person you truly are by dealing with past issues and helping you to see them as they truly are. Platform takes you through your life changes and helps you to face your inner fears.

This book is your best friend and confidant. By exploring your relationships in life and helping you to embrace them or do away with them; expect to be guided through your emotions and discover the solutions to your issues.

Embracing the person you have hidden within you for so many years and finding that lost child you left behind to grow up, you will be amazed at the talents and mysteries you begin to unlock about yourself. Grow your Platform though your journey and discover the natural driven passion you once thought was gone forever.

Part I

Too Much to Carry

I'm happy that you have decided today is the day you start your Platform journey. You deserve to be the true you inside and out. To hold your head up high and say **"world here I am"**.

These first few chapters help you to get familiar with the true person you are. What you have hiding within you that has long been waiting to come out. The true essence of the person you really are lies somewhere within your mind. It is trapped and fighting to make its way out.

Society, peers, family and your environment have caused you to suppress your true identity. Platform is here to help you find it. Find the person you really are and long to be.

We will guide you through this journey by helping you turn your disruptive and negative thinking into positive thoughts and reactions. By teaching you what clutters your mind and how to rid yourself of it. Also to help you figure out what triggers your negative way of thinking and how to disable it. We also focus on you learning to get out of your own way.

So get ready to start your Platform journey. No one can do it for you and you can't do it for anyone else. You must do it yourself!

CHAPTER 1

Clearing Your Mind

Often we tend to focus on things in our past and worry about things that haven't yet happened in our lives. Doing this causes us to feed our doubts and feeding our doubts delays our mind from the process of growth.

"If the mind is cluttered with emotions of the past and worries for the future then growth is inconclusive in the present."

Clearing your mind may seem like an impossible task but it really isn't. Embracing this step is the beginning of a life changing move. Putting your worries of what has yet to

Platform

come and constant thoughts of the past behind you will improve your present way of thinking.

Constantly, we worry about bills that have not arrived, family issues, our health, and dead end jobs, things from our childhood and what people think of us. Never once do we stop to think about the physical day we're living in, "the here and now."

This cluttering of our mind can go on for years causing more problems in our lives than necessary. Building up so much negativity in the way we think of ourselves and how we live. The negativity blocks us from seeing a solution to minor situations that arise. Everything then becomes a major problem and an instant worry.

By the time we realize what's transpiring in and around us; our clutter is at an ultimate high. Every day, we add more and more turmoil that we hit the extreme high of worries and doubts. Becoming so engrossed in negative thinking can drown you emotionally and psychologically. This strain on the mind makes it harder to gain control of yourself leaving you with a sense of hopelessness. If you don't clear your mind this will result in tragedy. You will be mentally lost in the clutter you created, stuck and making it harder to dig your way out.

I've been a worry wart for the majority of my young life up until I was ready to commit myself. Letting things that weren't in my control and the act of comparing myself to others made me feel less of a person. Let's talk about worries. I worried every time a bill was due and after I paid them guess what; there was another in its place.

In my neighborhood we had PSE&G for our heat and electric. Every time I would hear the truck I would run to the window and peek out, worrying if they were coming

Clearing Your Mind

to shut my lights off. The crazy part would be I had paid my bill. This went on for years. My panic attacks grew and so did my ulcers.

This was only one of my issues. I let other things build up inside me, little things, like annoying people that wouldn't leave me alone; dead end jobs where advancement was impossible. All of these emotions piled up on top of spreading my finances and life too thin and all because I didn't know how to clear my mind. I began to sink!

The clincher there is I never stopped to live. I worried myself sick trying to make ends meet and take care of my son. I lost myself, heck I was speeding doing 125mph in a 5mph zone of life.

Now that I have gone on my journey I have a lot of that under control. I have gotten married and added more children to the mix but I know how to clear my mind. This journey is an everyday lifelong practice. Doing it only once doesn't mean it's done and over with.

Every day we change as a person growing more and more so our platform journey is never truly over. Here you will learn how to have control of it. Note that you will always need to practice it.

Relax. You have time to save yourself. Depending on what stage of clutter you're in this transformation could happen quickly or could take weeks, months perhaps years to resolve.

Sit down and get focused! Chose a quiet moment where you have time to yourself. Somewhere without distractions no television, music, kids or noise. You need to give this activity your undivided attention. Prepare yourself you're about to enter what I call the danger zone.

Platform

The human mind is quite a complicated piece of equipment. It has good intentions and wants to rationalize but it jumps ahead and around our clutter without warning. Sometimes the mind produces multiple photographic images of old issues and new ones. Then it starts jumbling them together causing confusion and frustration.

The mind also has help it's a side kick called the heart. The heart plays a major part in decision making and can make sidetracks. These sidetracks cause you to lose focus and veer off course. Producing negative and empathetic emotions which can gain you the same results more clutter. Because of these emotions be careful and make sure you are in complete control of your mind. This is a meeting your heart should not attend.

For those of us whom walk by faith here is a little prayer to get you started. Having a guiding light to back you up and carry you when you fall doesn't hurt.

<u>**I PRAY FOR GOD TO PROVIDE ME WITH THE GIFT OF SIGHT AND TO LET ME HEAR WITH CLARITY. I'M PRAYING TO YOU OH LORD TO REMOVE THE CLUTTER FROM MY MIND. CARRY ME WHEN I AM WEAK AND SPEAK FOR ME WHEN MY WORDS WANT TO FAIL ME. THANK YOU LORD.**
AMEN</u>

Clutter Stage

Within the human mind is a part of the brain and it is called consciousness. It stores a tremendous amount of information that is manifested into imagination, thought,

Clearing Your Mind

memory, will, perception, emotion, opinion, intellect and sanity. Some of this information can overwhelm us by becoming a burden or an enlightenment affecting our everyday thoughts. Our thoughts are transposed into positive or negative energy based on our response to the way we process this information.

The information we collect in the mind can be easily divided into stages. **This is my way of breaking down the mind this is not a true scientific breakdown.** The stage I would like to focus on is the clutter stage. The clutter stage is a focus of the process of the mind.

To simplify the process even more I would like to break the clutter stage into two separate categories. I do this because putting it into two simplified categories is less discouraging than the several categories it truly consists of.

Although the clutter stage is flowing with nonstop information breaking it down into the categories of litter and baggage help weed out the unnecessary trash we are harboring.

Let me explain these categories. The litter category is the easiest to clear from your mind. This is all the unconnected issues you have lingering around like new things that have popped up that you can't stop thinking of. Maybe you've met someone new and you don't really like them or there's a job you want to apply for but you don't think you will be interviewed. These things are considered litter.

Next we have the baggage category. This is the hardest and most difficult of the two categories. Baggage is nothing but litter that has gotten out of control. These are the thoughts and feelings that have been festering like a sore and multiplying like ragweed. Microscopic parasites

Platform

that have been feeding on your emotional state of being and wearing away at your physical energy; so much they begin to have personalities of their own.

Create Your List

Begin by composing a list of your clutter. That would be the issues that are bothering you in the present, concerns of your future and worries of your past. It can be from your past as far back as when you were five and your brother pushed you down leaving you with a nasty scar or as recent as someone leaving the cap off of the tooth paste this morning. List all of your frustrations, worries and doubts. By the time your list is complete it will be long. Some of us may have to take a few days to complete this list and that's fine too. The mind has a remarkable amount of storage capacity. You will start to think of things you thought were long forgotten. It's not that they got resolved and cleared it's that they were buried amongst the muck of your other clutter.

Feeling the sense of being overwhelmed yet? Well put the list away until tomorrow. Don't do anything to the list. Writing all your issues down was enough for a day or three however long it takes you. It would be too much to look at and try to figure out what to do with it right now.

The next day or in three days, no longer than that pick up the list again during your quiet time. This should be the best time of day when you can focus and have a moment to be alone. Looking it over you will be able to easily see your issues front and center. Notice that some of

Clearing Your Mind

the issues will pretty much be the same or similar to each other. Put them into either the litter or the baggage categories this will allow you to see what your simple and major issues are.

Over time you will notice how you let your situations build up so much that they created smaller issues. These issues have caused you to not be focused on the present. They made your thought process inadequate leaving you incapable of solving simple issues.

Seeing everything on paper and categorizing it helps you to not only start clearing your mind but to devise a solution to your issues instead of placing a temporary bandage on them.

Platform

Process to Clearing Your Mind: Step 1

1. Prepare yourself to face your clutter.

2. You need quite time when your thoughts are the sharpest and most logical.

3. Make a list. Find out what your clutter is.

4. Put it away until the next day.

5. Categorize your clutter. Make no more than five sections.

6. Rationally find solutions to your clutter. Note that not all clutter will have permanent solutions some will need band aides until they arise again.

7. Repeat.

CHAPTER 2

Change the Way You Think

So many times we sit back and let our thoughts consume us. We tend to think too much. In our over thinking we create unforeseen scenarios usually starting and ending with negative outcomes. Sometimes it's hard to think positive when we are so use to defeat. Have you ever thought that if you changed the way you think, your defeated mentality will become a thing of the past?

When we fill ourselves with negative thoughts whether we speak them or think them we begin to believe them. Not only do these negative thoughts affect our way of thinking but they predict the outcome of our future actions.

Platform

"Embracing negative thoughts equals negative results."

Changing the way you think requires much practice. This change doesn't happen overnight. The reason being we are habitual by nature.

Over the course of our lives we are subconsciously conditioned by family, friends, peers and society. These outside influences tell us and make us believe that something is too hard for us to do and on the inside we begin to create an attitude of I can't do it. This "I can't" attitude is emotionally crippling and keeps some of us from producing positive reactions.

Where some people find the "I can't" attitude a game changer and it pushes them to produce a positive reaction, others let it fester negative thoughts and linger in them. They fall victim to the statement leaving them to desert their dreams, goals, furthering their education or even finding love in a relationship.

The way you think has a tremendous affect on what you attract into your life. How someone thinks of things changes their emotions and connects them to either accomplishing or hinders them from obtaining their goal.

For example one who thinks they will never find what they are destined to do most likely will never find it. Needless to say most won't even begin to research their inner selves to find what they are meant to do. One reason being they have already set up a mental block that keeps them from putting the initiative forward to start their search.

Change the Way You Think

Some however do begin their journey with positive thoughts and emotions but somewhere down the line they hit a mental block or a snag in their path. This snag causes dismay. Figuring they are kidding themselves and can't do it, they create a wall of negativity just as they begin to scratch the surface.

I, myself had fallen victim over and over again to my way of thinking. Just as I would start my life changing tasks I would hit that dreaded snag. It encouraged my doubts instead of fueling my eagerness. See not only did I dread the snag but I created a spot for it to grow. Before starting my journey I always had the "what if" scenarios. Believe me I had mainly bad what if's. Well a few steps into my journey when things were going great the "what if" would peek out and self doubt would begin to set in.

First, it would bring a broom then a chair and after that a light. Note that the broom was there to sweep all the previous positive thoughts out of the way. The chair gave the doubts a place to get comfortable and stay awhile. While the light helped for it to shine through everything I had fought to ignore.

The doubts only grew because I thought of those "what ifs". I showed them inside and they stayed. As little things came up I would say "see this is why I shouldn't have done this". All that did was make my doubts stronger and provide growth until my negative thinking was at an all time high.

When you hit this snag or mental block you must not let that put you off track. Time and time again throughout your journey you will encounter bumps in the road. Your reaction to these minor situations will make or break your

Platform

outcome. Giving in and up to early will result in more baggage or litter in your life.

So flush out those bad elements and ways of thinking and keep focused on the goal ahead. Everyday look back on yesterday's actions and reflect on the negative thought you had then turn it into a positive thought and reaction. Take note of when and what triggers your negative thinking. This way you can avoid it in the present and future.

Triggers

We all have emotional triggers that affect our thought process. Triggers can be anything that creates joyous emotions to emotions that make us angry wanting to spit fire. Triggers go off like a shot gun causing us to erupt into action.

Recognizing good and bad triggers in the beginning can be hard but once you start to notice what things, people and comments send you into a happy mood or spark a negative spiral you won't forget.

The very first "ah ha" moment is beautiful when it happens and most invigorating when you catch it on the regular and don't get upset. When we reach the, "negative ah ha" moment for the first time and don't know how to fix it the emotion of anger sets in. Quickly we get frustrated and fill displaced with our actions.

This displacement adds fuel to the fire of confusion stirring up a consistent flow of negative energy. That negative energy builds up forming our negative thoughts and without time to filter it, it produces catastrophic

Change the Way You Think

reactions. It is wise that when you have reached a "*bad* ah ha" moment you stop and walk away from it.

Removing yourself from that irritating moment is not cowardly it is the smartest thing you can do. You must take time to regroup and replace the negative thought with a positive thought. Finding the silver lining in a bad situation is always best to defeat your negative emotions. Remember that these bad situations are negative triggers that keep you from having a positive reaction.

Just as there are bad triggers we also have good triggers. Good triggers are what we long for. These should be sought out just know you can never have too many good triggers in my book.

When you have the first good "ah ha" trigger moment, addiction will set in immediately. You will start to crave more of these positive thoughts and changing the way you think can produce more of these emotions. Shortly after encountering these happy triggers you will notice a mental then a physical change with yourself.

Mentally you become undefeatable more knowledgeable to the things you truly want in life. Physically your posture will change and your voice becomes a little louder and more direct. You stand just a little taller and talk with more confidence each day especially when you have a consistent flow of good triggers.

Bad triggers are altered into good triggers and can be recognized when you are confident with a little bit of conceit heck a lot if you have it. Can you name one successful person who is not confident and conceited in their demeanor?

To be successful and build your platform you must be confident in your own skin. If you are not confident but

Platform

pretend to be people will notice right away. When I say skin I am talking about you as an entire person mind, body and soul. The way you think reflects on the way you carry yourself on the inside and outside of your body.

Not only must you change the way you think you must change the way you think of yourself. In order to start this process you must first have in practice Step 1 from the previous chapter which is "Clearing Your Mind". Without having that step in practice Step 2 won't work.

Change the Way You Think

Process to Change the Way You Think: Step 2

1. Start complementing yourself each time you pass a mirror.

2. Take notice of your good and bad triggers.

3. Reflect on yesterday's negative thoughts and change them in to positive actions.

4. Embrace your good "ah ha" moments and look for more of those.

5. Repeat.

CHAPTER 3

Get Out of Your Own Way

As children we are taught many things. From the moment we first open our eyes we soak up life lessons without questioning them or trying to dissect them. In other words we adapt well to the sponge effect without having to be learn how to retain what we are being taught.

Unfortunately some things are harder than others for our parents to teach us or for us to catch on to. Even as we grow older and begin learning life lessons in our early school age years our teachers can't even teach us some things.

One thing I hope to bring to light and teach you is "How to get out of your own way". You may not know it but we stand in our own way the majority of our lives. Most

Platform

of us just don't know it. I came to the realization one day that it can be so easy for someone standing in our way to move just by us saying two simple words "excuse me". Believe me I say excuse me every time I'm in the grocery store. On record it has to be about fifteen to twenty times every trip.

If others can move out of our way so easily just by us asking than why is it so hard for us to get out of our own way, when trying to move forward? The simple words of excuse me won't work on ourselves or will it?

"To stand in our own way is to drown in our own vision."

Throughout all parents' struggles and adversities in life one would think that they would know to teach their children how to get out of their own way. They surely teach us how to let people know to move out of our way.

Being a parent myself I seriously had to stop and think about this for a minute. If my parents didn't think to teach me to do this, I must find away to teach my children how to do this.

Let's face it, I figured if I could teach them this tactic, they would have more time practicing until it became second nature. Giving your children a jump on this, among other platform building skills, will insure they move through life taking more positive initiatives. Using their God given instinct and keeping it instead of letting the outcries of society dictate what they are capable and not capable of doing.

Get Out of Your Own Way

As I pondered over this for weeks on end I would stand in front of the bathroom mirror repeating "excuse me miss". Yes you all, I know this sounds crazy but hey I had to figure this out.

Frustration sat in as I knew I had the answer on the tip of my tongue. In fact the very root of the problem was hiding in the dark and poking its ugly head out at me. Day in and day out it was like a scavenger hunt trying to pin point the exact thought I had when I first felt the answer trying to come to me. A few more days went by and I had to walk away from the issue. The excuse me villain had escaped my capture.

Needless to say it was time to go grocery shopping again and I prepared myself for the endless repeating of "excuse me" I would be passing out. Zipping through the aisles I had excused myself so much by the end of my trip I wanted to shout.

By the time I reached checkout small talk was out of the question. While waiting in line I didn't hear this young lady behind me say excuse me. I proceeded to put my things on the conveyor belt and threw everything in my basket hurriedly so I could head for my truck. Before I could push the cart completely out of the aisle I heard a lady behind me say I said excuse me to her I was trying to just get pass. I turned and realized she was talking about me. I didn't know at the time she was talking to me and I surely didn't know I was in her way.

After tossing the groceries into the truck I sat in the driver seat and mumbled to myself for a while. Furious and annoyed I sat there thinking. How was I to know I was in her way? Then I looked into the rearview mirror and realized "I got it". It was like Christmas in July I had finally

Platform

figured it out, the answer to the very question that bothered me for weeks was staring me right in the face.

How could someone know to get out of their own way if they don't know they're standing in their own way? Finally, I could hold my head up high knowing that I have solved a riddle that haunted me and many others.

See, to get out of your own way you must first acknowledge that you are standing in your way. You must realize the difference from someone else keeping you from something you want to achieve and when you are the person blocking yourself from what you want. That's the first step in solving the issue.

Most times we have no idea that we are standing in our own way. Catching ourselves as being the culprit is one of the most daunting things to do. It takes sometime and getting use to. Usually the notion of I can't do it, this is too hard or just creating excuses of why we shouldn't pursue something we love to do are concrete signs that we're blocking ourselves.

This constant blockage will cause us to be down on ourselves about any and every positive thing that tries to alter our lives for the better. Things that will have a major impact to change our lives for the better will never come because we don't know how to say "excuse me" to ourselves.

Once we learn to get out of our own way we open many doors and windows of opportunity for ourselves. After acknowledging that we are standing in our own way we must now focus on excusing ourselves. This step may sound foolish but understand that it is necessary and no step is foolish when you're on your journey to a new platform of life.

Get Out of Your Own Way

Think of the things in life you love to do. The things that make you happy whether it is sewing, baking, doing taxes you name it, think of it. Make sure these are things you would like to experience and some are things you use to do as a child. Some may even be outrageous and possibly not economical for you at this point in your life. Don't worry that's okay. Just be sure to include those things in this exercise.

Some of you will have a broad list and some may only have five to ten different things and that's great. When learning to get out of your own way you have to start somewhere and starting with the things in life you would love to do is a great start.

One by one start to go down your list separating the things you would like to experience from the things you love doing. Next determine if any of the things you would love to do are a true passion. Maybe if you love working out, you may be a nutrition fanatic or you love gardening and would love to do that full time instead of the job you have now.

Try imaging you doing something you love to do every day and getting paid to do it. Aha! Now you're on to something. Possibly there is a new career you've been secretly suppressing and want to pursue and you have been standing in your own way and couldn't see it.

Perhaps after making your list you find out you've been longing for a vacation or want to go back to school but you've been telling yourself it's too expensive. Or you've been pining away after a new wardrobe but you just have too many bills. Well listen up to day is the day you start to make a change.

Platform

Look over all those things and next to them write the opposite of what you feel about the things you want or would love to do. For all of the reasons you say I can't you will now have I can and I will in their place.

If you don't conquer this list or attempt to put a dent in it you are at fault and are standing in your own way. Please do understand that not everything you said you would love to do is something you will quit your day job and just begin doing. On the other hand the one true passion that you have is the one that will start the tables turning. You will find that you have an unbelievable drive to make it happen once you've started it. It will come a time where you will have to decide to make it your full blown reality. The pursuit of happiness is inevitable and you are no exception to it.

So get out of your own way and let your passion shine threw. Don't let your dreams be decided by bills that won't go away and or people who don't believe in you or those that don't want to see you do better than them. Most importantly don't be your own evil villain standing in the mist waiting to destroy your true passion or goals in life.

Get Out of Your Own Way

Process to Get Out of Your Own Way: Step 3

1. Recognize that it's you standing in your own way and face yourself head on in the mirror.

2. Figure out what your passion, goals and what you want to experience in life (write them down).

3. Next to the list you gathered in step two make another column. For every thought of I can't write I will or I can.

4. Make a solution to how you will achieve each passion, goal or experience and write the plan on the back.

5. Repeat. *This list will constantly alter as you accomplish and venture on to new goals in life.

Part II

What Lies Underneath

Now that you have made it through part 1 the next best thing is to continue on your journey. To recap part one, you have learned to clear your mind, change the way you think, and how to get out of your own way. These steps I find are the most vital when starting your platform journey. They lay the very foundation of your inner true self.

Once you have completely dealt with the most emotional parts of yourself and the main person who stands in your way (you) you're able to move on and deal with what lies underneath.

As humans we are very complex. We are easily bruised by others words or actions, whether we chose to admit it or not. Being subject to these harsh emotions and actions of others can have positive and negative effects on us. It's up to us to choose how these negative effects will affect our well being and thinking.

In these next few chapters you will get to focus on the present. You will think about what would happen if you die today, how to look for motivation and how to learn from your past failures. I know I said we would focus on the present but you have to look at the past failures so you can learn what not to do in the present day. Failures don't repeat themselves, tries do.

You will also learn how to recognize and accept when you have outgrown friends. Know that outgrowing friends shows that you are achieving growth in your life. You are expanding your true inner self by adding onto your network of friends and not being afraid to close doors if and when necessary.

CHAPTER 4

If I Die Today

Too often we speed forcefully through life with many thoughts of the past and future but don't stop to think about today. Have you ever thought to yourself if I were to die today what would I have done with my life? Would I have done all the things I long to do? What legacy would I have to leave behind?

"If I die today then my life holds no value because I never seized the day. All my hopes and dreams fade away never to be accomplished by me."

It's sad to say but we do not think of things like this until our life is on the line. For instance we come close to a

Platform

near death experience, we see someone who is close to us dying or who has just died. Much too often we take our time here for granted. Leaving everything for tomorrow when we know tomorrow is not promised.

In my life time I was fortunate to have both of my great grandmothers around. One I didn't know so well because we didn't get to see her as often but the other was around all the time. Oh I enjoyed every moment of it. I spent many days with Nanny, my mother's grandmother. Boy was she a pistol. She took no shorts, demanded respect and was as sweet as they get (well she was to me).

See I was always interested in the stories of her life growing up and the struggles she went through to get where she ended up. At her funeral I began to wonder if she had lived the life she wanted, I know she made many sacrifices for the family. I wondered, did she die happy and was she fulfilled with her life? I was too young back then as a child to ask her and as I grew I hardly ever went to visit her anymore and the times that I did go her memory wasn't strong enough to tell me those stories. So I never bother to ask her those questions. I just enjoyed whatever time we had left.

I knew the day she died I would do everything I could to live my life the way I wanted the best way I could. Of course over time my mind, thoughts and society took over. Helping me to suppress those emotions of living life the way I wanted to. I had to pay bills and raise my kids. I didn't have time for dreams and goals.

Then one summer day the thought of not knowing what I wanted anymore hit me. I had become ordinary. Day by day I forgot about myself and became another crab in the pot, another grain of sand on the ocean floor.

If I Die Today

Nothing stood out. I hustled and bustled every day until I burned myself out and finally the job I once depended on was gone, over and I had nothing to say for it.

So I thought to myself if I died today what have I done with my life? Would I be happy with what I accomplished for myself? What examples have I set for my children to look at and say no matter what my mother accomplished her goals and turned her dreams into her reality.

For the majority of us our plights become our convictions and overrule our determination to conquer our goals and or dreams. Not only must we fight through these issues that arise, we must keep focus on the goal at hand. The goal would be to muster enough mental strength to surpass these dreadful plights so we aren't suffocating ourselves, digging future unforeseen traps of mental deception.

The long fight I have with myself still to this day is not letting the outside world change my personal design. If I die today I want to know that I lived my life, ran after my goals one by one and embodied my passion. We all must strive to make sure we are true to ourselves. We must live out and act upon what is natural to our DNA embed talents and not something that has been forced upon us by everyone else.

Setting forth with my passion and goals in place you would be shocked to know that I am a woman of many talents. Wearing multiple hats in life is my design and I don't fight it. I use to. I would always say the popular saying "a jack of all trades a master at none". I use to feel that that was written exactly for me and I would never find my true design; my true passion. Boy was I wrong and so

Platform

are you if you fill that way. Your design maybe to be a jack of all trades but if you don't investigate you can never be a master at any. Besides, it takes a long time to master something. I still haven't mastered walking and I've been doing that for over thirty years. I trip at the least three times a day.

Being the President, CEO of more than one company, author and mother is time consuming but I'm living my passions and accomplishing my goals. With all that on my plate I'm still searching for my next goal to conquer.

Many people will try to discourage you and you will even try to discourage yourself at times. When that happens and it will take a moment to reflect on your life and think to yourself if I die today would I have done all the things that I wanted and was designed to do?

If I Die Today

Process to If I Die Today: Step 4

    1. Time of Reflection.

    2. Repeat from time to time.

CHAPTER 5

Look For Motivation

Having a lack of motivation in our lives leaves us to being stagnant with how we pursue things of interest. Have you ever seen a donkey lose its motivation? It plops down right where it stands no matter what and getting it to move again is almost impossible.

"The act of motivation is a source from within longing to get out and become a thing of motion."

See the truth about the donkey being stubborn and showing a lack of motivation is true but for a reason other than laziness. It is part of their intelligence that makes them be cautious and they preserve themselves leaving us to

Platform

think they are lazy. Unlike the horse who takes flight when they are scared the donkey stops in its tracks to observe the situation and weighing it's options before taking the best approach and proceeding.

We are often like this but some of us get stuck in donkey mood and never get up again. You have to find what motivates you to carry on. You need to observe the situation as it is and take the best approach. It's okay to stop and observe your surroundings, accomplishments, failures and so on but not to get so wrapped up in them you stuck there.

At time we become so overwhelmed with the things around us that we tucker out quickly. In the beginning we jump at every opportunity we get without devising a plan that conquers and attack. When we become so overwhelmed our motivation dwindles. It's more like a candle slowly fading out.

Not only is it hard for us to see the positivity in what first motivated us, it is hard to find new motivation. Often times we have no idea of where to find or how to recapture the motivation we lost. So we must look for ways or people to create motivation.

Proceed with caution into where you look for motivation. You can try looking for inspiration from books, internet, television, friends, and family. Just know when you do look for motivation in these people or things you're going to be met with some resistance.

You can read as many books and watch as much positive television as you want. But once you close the book and turn the television off you're on your own. Now that you have enlightened your mind with that information you must put what you've learned to good use. If you can't

Look For Motivation

seem to find a way to use what you learned from those sources and find yourself still in donkey mode than you haven't recaptured your motivation and should continue your search.

As far as our friends and family are concerned they can be good and bad for our motivation. When it comes to those dear to us they mean well but can actually create more discouragement within us almost making our motivation for our desire fade into oblivion.

Let's just say when your family and friends see you trying different things and fail at them time and time again they will try to steer you in the opposite direction. Especially when you have an infamous track record of making it midway or almost to the end of your project then giving up, they latch on to that. It's not that they don't want to support you anymore. Most of the time they can't handle your roller coaster of enthusiasm, you're highs and lows when things are good but you get discouraged.

To many times their "you can do it attitude" turns into a "why don't you just stick to what is already working". You may even encounter them ignoring you or just giving you nonchalant responses during many conversations. Basically they can care less about another adventure you've decided to go on. In their minds you won't finish this one either so you're on your own.

It took me a while to figure this out. Why, you ask? Well I'm guilty of starting a project getting close to the end and never finishing. The lack of motivation I had always seemed to creep up on me like the music in a scary movie. I could always muster motivation in the beginning and get everyone excited. But when I hit the midpoint and a few

Platform

snags I would become so discouraged I would lose all of my motivation to push through.

So with my new adventures I couldn't really look to family and friends because no one was truly interested. They may not have said it but actions did reveal themselves. Heck they were tired of my roller coaster of motivation and they had every right to be. Let's face it I would start off with a great run and then next week I would be down in the dumps.

Motivation is best tackled alone. You are your best asset to having true self-assured motivation. That's why one should not seek their motivation through the thoughts of others and rely on what they feel about what you're doing.

There needs to be a number one cheerleader on your team. That cheerleader is YOU! If you are in need of a secondary source of motivation *(which is fine because most of us need one)* just make sure that is has no personal or emotionally attachment to you. This helps you to deter any unwanted negative emotions you can encounter from family or friends.

Don't get me wrong some friend and family encouragement is great but don't look for them to be your motivational priority or pivot.

Look For Motivation

Process to Look for Motivation: Step 5

1. Try to remember what it is about what you're doing that inspired you to take on the task in the first place.

2. Weed out the unwanted discouragement in your life.

3. Look for positive encouragement. Be your #1 cheerleader!

4. Repeat for every task you encounter.

CHAPTER 6

Learn From Your Failures

Failure is a word that makes us cringe when we hear it. When our name is attached to our failures we tend to want to go and hide under a rock. People have become so obsessed with being let down by their failures they forget to embrace them. That sounds ridiculous but embracing these temporary let downs and facing them puts you further ahead in achieving success.

"Our failures are our gateways to achieving suppressed goals that have undetermined future and success."

Platform

Facing one's failures is one of the hardest things to do in life next to trying new things. These two acts go hand in hand. If one does not try something new one will never know the senses of defeat or failure. Not experiencing defeat or failure is next to not experiencing life at all.

I'm not saying you have to live on the edge and try every daring thing that you come across or participate in every adventure that rolls past you. But you must try to embark on new experiences especially the ones that have your interest.

As we tread through life we experience failures without even realizing it. When you were a toddler you had to learn to walk and suffer through potty training. If you would have had an option to fail and not try again you may be rolling instead of walking and wearing a diaper right now. Instead without you even knowing it you embraced your failures and with the help of some over eager loved one you overcame this experience.

The point is you had and experienced. You learned what to do and what not to do from your failure and accomplished the goal you set out to conquer. It doesn't matter how many times you had to attempt the task the only thing that matters is you defeated the task.

Time and time again we are teased throughout life when we fail. It becomes an underwritten statement which we sulk about. We must walk with our tail between our legs and hang our head in shame, when it is just the opposite.

Know I hate to fail but it is a process of life everyone must go through in order to be successful. I spent most of my young life feeling like a failure until I took a stand and looked at things differently. I realized some time ago that if you haven't failed you haven't learned a thing. It took time

Learn From Your Failures

for me to come to this realization. I was letting my failures beat me up. They were keeping me hostage. I wasn't able to move on to other things or try to experience what I had failed at again because of shame.

Yes, shame! Failure is nothing but shame. I talked to my mother one day about failing so many times at different things. Of course she gave me the good old speech of "nothing beats a failure but a try." She would always say this to me but for some reason this time it stuck out.

Quietly the wheels started turning in my head if I keep trying maybe I will get pass this moment. So upon my many downfalls I decided to embark on my new journey and write books again. I bet you didn't see this one coming.

Previously I had written a book but my flash drive had caught a virus. I was so heartbroken it took me an entire year to recuperate from the disappointment of my failure of not being able to put the book out I had talked about for months. After that long dreadful year past I was ready to listen to my mother and try again.

This time my new book was flowing out of my brain even faster than my first book. Then my doubt kicked in and my failure temperature started to rise and before I knew it I had stopped writing yet again. Only this time nothing had caught a virus. I couldn't figure out what was going on.

I sat for a few weeks and sulked around the house. My kids stared at me my husband tried to give me inspiration but I couldn't see what was going on until a few nights later during our many talks. I had blurted out "I don't want to fail." Wow I didn't even see that coming when I had said it.

Platform

I went on and on telling him about all my past failures and how I didn't want to fail at this to. After I vented I felt like a weight was lifted off of my chest. That's when I knew I was letting my failure run and ruin my life.

Not only had I let my failures stand in my way, they started to rule my life. This was the first time I stood tall and took my failures head on. No longer would they be my fear but they would be my experience. They became life and experience building moments I could speak on and relay to my audience as I did with my colleagues and friends.

So we all have to fight our many journeys and fighting through our failures and facing them is just another step. We must learn from them in order to proceed forward and be successful.

Learn From Your Failures

Process to Learn From Your Failures: Step 6

1. Take your past failures and turn those into the fuel that pushes you to do accomplish your next goal.

2. Analyze what makes you feel ashamed of your failures.

3. Take small steps into conquering your failure by trying the task again.

4. Embrace your failures as life lessons.

5. Repeat.

CHAPTER 7

Outgrowing Friends Is a Process of Growth

As we grow older we are suppose to grow as people. Sometimes that means we end up leaving our friends behind. It's not that we don't love them anymore or that we want nothing to do with them, it's just we've grown a part and are going in different directions.

"Sometimes we must let go of our loved ones in order to grow and reach our higher self."

Often we look to our friends for guidance and support throughout our lives. We hope to create everlasting

Platform

bonds that will stand the test of times, well some do and some don't. It's good to remember that some people enter our lives for short to long term reasons. Many are here to teach us a quick lesson and some a lifelong lesson.

In many cases we end up giving people the title of friend before they have truly earned that right to be in our hearts. Friends are gifts you give yourself. That's what my mother taught me. We walk through our younger years looking for that special bond. Unfortunately we don't stop to scrutinize who really deserves to have that title in our lives. It's usually when we come into our adulthood that we start to pick people apart.

When I say adulthood I mean maturity not age. See by law you are considered an adult between the ages of 18-21. What I'm referring to is maturity and that doesn't hit most of us until we hit our mid to late thirties. At that time our outlook on life is changing and so is our mindset in a whole. We start to realize the importance of family and the security of a job or career. Most of us have a hunger inside and we don't know what it is until we start our new life journey. This is the time we look to find out the five W's of our life {who, what, where, why, when and how}. Constantly we find ourselves in deep thought trying to find meanings to the simplest things and what we want out of life.

Life becomes a little smothering at some points. We notice what we could tolerate before is an irritating nuisance to us now. Most of the time we look at the people whether family or friends that surround us and notice the negative or positive emotions they bring to us. Even if there are negative emotions we try to find the bright side to

Outgrowing Friends Is a Process of Growth

having them around not realizing the effect they are having on our positivity.

So many of us get wrapped up in our friendships that we are willing to keep ourselves stationary in life just to appease our friends. While more and more we drown in the misery we're living and the feeling of despair because we can't sever a bond that has grown weak. For this feeling, we have no one to blame but ourselves.

We subject ourselves to hanging on to friendships that don't help us grow but continuously drain our energy. In many cases the other party has no idea what you are going through. Remember when you experience this in your friendship you need to be honest with yourself. You need to think of what is best for you. Ruffling a few feathers helps to weed out the meaningful and wasteful relationships you have. Sometimes you need to remove yourself for a while or just end the friendship all together.

It is a hard thing to do as I have experienced it first hand and it seemed to hit me all at once. I knew that if I truly was the other person's friend and our friendship was meant to be we would meet again further down the road. Not many people accept this but to live a successful life you will lose and gain friends along your journey. You have to do what's best for you.

During our lives people come and go and so do friends. It is a process of growth that we all must go through. If you chose to ignore this process you will suffer from endless doubts about yourself and where you're going in your life. You have to be honest and true to yourself even though it means you and another person or many people may experience some pain of separation.

Platform

Don't worry you are not being selfish although they will make you feel like you are. Whatever you do know that you are doing this for you and you're personal growth.

Sometimes friends run their course and become acquaintances. They may not like their new position but that is the position you have available. If they want to be a part of your life they will accept it no matter what. You're not replacing them. Instead for the first time in your adulthood you are appreciating you and your needs.

When we out grow the people in our lives it doesn't mean new people won't enter. It means we now know what we want and we finally understand what we need in a friendship. So when the next one comes along understand the friendship may not last forever but you will appreciate the lesson you learn from each person that enters your life.

Outgrowing Friends Is a Process of Growth

Process to Outgrowing Friends Is a Process of Growth: Step 7

1. Do a quick scan of your friendships. Think about your relationship with them.

2. Decide whether it is positive or negative emotions you experience with them.

3. The people that create pure negative emotions and you know that's not where you want to be, you should make the decision if you have outgrown them or if you can ignore their negativity and successfully achieve your platform of success.

4. Repeat this process as new people come into and exit your life

CHAPTER 8

Don't Be Afraid To Close Doors

The very thought of change can bring us to our knees. Crying out like babies looking for our mother and father to come and make everything better. Well that's not how life works. Our lives change on a dime everyday and at any given moment for no rhyme or reason it just does. Sometimes we are forced to close doors so new beginnings can arise in their place.

"If you've been loyal to one concept and haven't experienced anything new don't be afraid to close the door and try something."

Closing doors in our lives aren't easy. But when we seek new experiences hoping to better ourselves it is a must. Putting our fears aside to close these doors means

Platform

putting our security at risk. This could be the security of our job in order to venture out for a new job or leaving our old lives behind us to look for something much more fulfilling.

When it's time to close doors our fear becomes a big factor. The fear we have for new beginnings will cause us to halt in our footsteps that slow down any progress we have or are looking to make. Fear is a big factor in destroying our ambition to take the next step in life. Learning to control fear takes time and practice.

Being afraid to close doors can keep us from the very thing we desire in life. For example coming face to face with a relationship that is going nowhere, we know it, but are too afraid to move out of our comfort zone. This is what poses the problem.

Think about dating someone that you like but you know they are not what you're looking for. You may have been together for a few years and you're comfortable with one another. Moving on is the furthest from your mind. Even if you both decide to date other people you feel you must kept a line of communication open. You refuse to close the door because you are afraid.

You're not afraid of finding Mr. or Mrs. Right. You're afraid that if you let your safety net go and you don't find the next best thing, you'll be all alone. You will feel you've closed the door on your comfort zone. When we think we've closed the door on our comfort zone the longing sensation for the relationship will hinder us from moving forward.

The longing sensation is a reflection of your fear. We all know when you can't erase their phone number or can't delete them from your social media page. For some odd

Don't Be Afraid To Close Doors

reason you just can't let go. Even though you say you closed the door you didn't. So now you can kiss the thought of finding Mr. or Mrs. Right goodbye.

Consciously you must decide to put your foot down and not be afraid. Letting go of whatever is holding you back and keeping you stagnant in life is a must. Closing doors has to occur in order for new doors to open.

For many years I worked at the same job with no room for growth or advancement. I knew deep down inside I was meant for something more but being a single mom it was my only security. I was too afraid to step out on my faith and close the door to find what was meant for me in my life. Not closing this door after realizing my life was at a dead stop didn't help.

In fact I became miserable and irritable. As time went on and I couldn't understand why everyone around me was doing well with their lives and I couldn't seem to catch a break. Every opportunity that I would get to apply for a new job I would put it off. Waiting until the next time someone made me angry at the job or I felt underappreciated.

Never once did I stop to think I was the one making myself feel underappreciated. I was hurting myself because I wouldn't let go of my safety net. So afraid to close the door on the one job that I had that gave me flexibility to an extent to raise my son but barley gave me enough money to pay the bills. I would think what was I to do?

It wasn't until about four years of slowly sinking into misery I had been in a relationship for awhile and was happy. My fiancé and I had decided it was time I left the job before I had a heart attack. My son and future stepson were tired of me coming home angry and exhausted.

Platform

This job not only became a burden on me but my family was suffering. Shortly after I had given my notice I felt I made the worst decision ever to leave my job not to mention I found out I was pregnant after the fact.

It seemed like my life was falling apart. One thing after another started to go. I lost two cars in that month and my lights were shut off. Not only was one door closing it seemed like my life was closing down too.

Being afraid to close doors in my life had taken a toll on me. My fear build up and I made desperate decisions still leaving the door to that job open for me if I needed it in the future. For two years after that I suffered from leaving that door open.

It took me moving two hours away to start to see things clearly. I finally found the courage to face my fear and say to myself I'm not going back to that job. Once I acknowledged my fear and wasn't afraid to close the door I started finding it was easier to close many other doors.

After about six months things started to rapidly change doors opened for me and I began to think clearly about life. Other opportunities start to appear. The first opportunity didn't come in the form of a job but a vacation. For the first time in six years I was able to go on a vacation.

It wasn't until I was on vacation that I finally understood that my fear of closing doors was preventing me from living. That day forward I knew that closing doors only led to other doors opening. They may not be the doors you want but they are the doors you need at that time in your life.

Don't Be Afraid To Close Doors

So don't be afraid to close doors. Keeping doors open that have been open to long will prolong you from your intended growth.

Platform

Process to Don't Be Afraid to Close Doors: Step 8

1. Think about what doors you've have left open that need to be closed.

2. Figure out what you need to do to close the doors.

3. One by one close them.*Make sure if it is a job you have another alternative lined up.

4. Repeat throughout your journey.

Part III

Bringing Fourth Your Platform

Let's get ready to bring fourth your platform and kiss the old you goodbye. By now you have been through a very difficult and emotional roller coaster. Your mind has been worked out and stripped of its former way of thinking. You can now begin focusing on the new you that's waiting to emerge.

Throughout your journey many changes have risen and your way of thinking and your outlook on life is now different. You have planted a seed in your mind that has made you feel that anything and everything your heart desires and believes is for you is attainable.

In the next few chapters we focus on saying goodbye to the old you and your old ways by showing you how to embrace the new and improved you. The person that has been lost in the shadows of your mind because of society and peers thoughts of how you should or should not be is about to be set free.

So let's put on those big girl panties and your big boy shorts and face your fears. As we face your fears we will act on turning them into accomplishments and help you put the plans together to make it happen.

No worries you will do just fine because you are going to learn that you must jump and take chances and never settle in order to continuously grow your Platform.

CHAPTER 9

Kissing the Old You Goodbye

As we grow throughout our life journey we encounter one of our biggest battles and that is when and how to kiss the old us goodbye. It's hard to recognize when our new self wants to emerge because of our unconscious battle with our old self.

However we will see changes within our character, the way we react to familiar situations and how we address conflict. Although those changes are clear to us we still refuse to acknowledge our new self.

"Seeking and achieving growth means ridding our lives of our former selves."

Platform

Our battle within is serious. When we're looking to take on new traits and change our character to something our conscious mind is not use to we encounter an internal war. It depends on the person themselves to figure out how long their war is going to last. To many times we let the battle go on for so long that our new self seems to fade away or get mixed in with the our old self.

It is best to take on your new self immediately as you start to practice and change your way of thinking. If you accept your new self and let the old you know there's a new sheriff in town, your battle won't be as hard as you think.

Most of us find it quite hard to accept change. When we deny ourselves change we stop our growth. No matter if your five years old or ninety-nine years old you will continue to grow as a person. Every day we are alive and breathing we are growing. With every new encounter we subject ourselves to bring on new adventures, new ways of thinking, reacting to new, different or similar situations but in new ways. These encounters help our minds to grow and form us into the person we are.

As for myself I was a negative thinker since I was a child. I lived this way for a long time miserable and under motivated. I didn't like to have much contact with people and always suffered for thinking I didn't belong. Not only was I negative but I was confusing because my actions didn't always reflect my thoughts.

Entering into young adulthood I changed somewhat but not much. I still continued with negative thoughts toward myself and didn't care for much contact with people. The difference was my negative thoughts and actions started to match up perfectly and shortly after embracing this way of life I started down a dark path.

Kissing the Old You Goodbye

There's a time where we all have to wake up and see our life as it truly is. There isn't a thing in our lives that can't be changed but you must learn to kiss the old you goodbye so you can embrace the new you.

It took having a child for my life to change and me to recognize that the person I was needed to change. So I began my transformation. I began to think with positivity and those thoughts help me to produce positive reactions.

After seeing myself in a new way I knew and felt better than I had ever felt I knew that's who I wanted to be from then on. My outlook on life had change I loved myself and realized I didn't have to be negative about everything. I didn't let societies issues with being a single mother out of wedlock deter me from being the new me.

Yes, it is possible for you to do it too! You don't have to have a child for you to kiss your old self goodbye. While on this journey don't let the person that was so negative about every aspect of life have any control. Turn every negative into a positive. No matter what remember for every negative reaction there is a positive reaction. You just have to find it.

When someone tries to anger you don't let them. Know that you have the control over your feelings. The old you would get upset and want to seek revenge but the new you has no time for foolishness and chooses to move on.

You must look at the old you as flawed, insecure and a bad thorn. In some cases you can compare yourself to the rotten food left in the refrigerator after a month. Now let's be even more realistic try to think of the stench being magnified from birth until now. You would want to burn down that refrigerator and get a new one right?

Platform

Well you don't have to burn anything down. You just need to "LET GO"! Let go of the old you. It will take some time but keep practicing.

Kissing the Old You Goodbye

Process of Kissing the Old You Goodbye: Step 9

1. See the change in yourself.

2. Accept the changes you are making in your life. The new thoughts and reactions you are bringing forth.

3. Every time you are confronted with a negative thought or action bring forth the new you.

4. Practice the new you often.

5. Repeat these steps whenever needed.

CHAPTER 10

Embracing the New You

Hi and welcome to the new you. Yes! You are ready to embrace the personality that has been cocooned within you and trying to burst its way out. This is a proud moment. Once you are ready to unleash the new you, you can begin building your platform.

"At some point we must embrace the new personality within us so we can build our platform or suffer from a stained identity."

Just as you have to learn new things you have to learn how to embrace the new you. It takes us time for our mind and body to accept that there's a change coming.

Platform

Especially, when we make the choice that changing from our former selves is what we want. The immediate reaction of rejection is normal. But when you make a conscious choice to embrace the new person you are becoming, it helps the process to move along with fewer hiccups.

Every day you need to practice your new behavior and habits. Instead of having quick and predictable retaliations to things that affect you in negative ways, you need to stop and take a step back. Stop and analyze the situation in front of you before speaking or reacting.

Maybe you need to be assertive or keep your composure in this situation. You can't make a clear decision without stepping back and observing. One part of embracing the new you is practicing observation before reaction.

It takes having control over your former self so that you are able to make rational decisions. Deprogramming yourself from all the years of being told to act a certain way or being told what you can or can't achieve are still within you. The act of fighting them and conquering the emotions are all in practicing embracing your new behavior and way of thinking.

Not only is your mind learning to embrace the new you but so is your body. See some people don't understand you must change the inside before you change the outside to make sure you don't fall subject to what is on the inside. If you haven't fixed what's on the inside then the outside is irrelevant.

Take for instance you are shopping for a new home. You come across this wonderful Victorian colonial. The outside has a beautiful wraparound porch and it's been painted and has strong standing pillars on the front that

Embracing the New You

stand out against the neighbors boring old homes. Let's not forget the curb appeal that brings you in wanting to run through the front door screaming where do I sign?

Upon entering the home your smile becomes distorted and turns into an immediate frown as you gaze upon the inside. The entry way has peeling paint and stains on the floor. Old mail is tossed in the corner that is filled with spider webs. You don't give up you decide you can deal with that it's not so bad especially because the outside is so gorgeous. You press on walking through each room. It seems the deeper you get into the house the worst the house gets. Big holes are in the walls and one room has no ceiling at all. You're on your way to the kitchen when a slight warm summer breeze kisses your cheek. Your mind thinks maybe a window is open. It's funny how we try to rationalize things especially when our first perception is filled with such bliss.

Entering into the kitchen you're shocked. It is not like the first few rooms you encountered. In fact most of it is intact and painted. But there is a breeze coming in and you can feel it. As you head over in the direction of the breeze the floor slopes sort of like a hill. You also notice the window is open just a bit. As you try to close the window the wall gives way and falls backward into a yard fill with garbage and old furniture.

So many of us fall victim to thinking we can change the outside first and work on our internal struggles later. When we do this we set ourselves up for failure. See they tell you to fake it till you make it but they don't tell you the steps that come before that. When you create a false perception of yourself and you haven't done any repair work on the inner you that perception doesn't get to manifest naturally.

Platform

The mind feels tricked and you feel worse than you did before.

That's why we have been working on your mind not tricking it but fixing it. You must endure the struggles of the mind before you can change the outside. The outside is nothing without the inside. The outside does not represents what is going on inside. It's the supporting role not the main role.

Outside Appearance

As you push to getting your new behavior and personality to shine through you will start to look at the outer appearance. Not just the materialistic parts but the aspects of your life, career, relationships, goals and dreams. Those are just some the things you will start to want to conquer in your platform quest.

These outside appearances aren't there just for show. They are a part of the new you. Consisting of the things you thought you couldn't do, things you were too afraid to face and mostly the possibilities that you put on the back burner.

The fears you once held in you can now become accomplishments. Why and how you ask? Well you will now face them head on by developing a plan of action. You will take the chance when offered opportunities that may never come up again, follow your passion and never settle for something negative that you can change into a positive.

When you have changed your inner self, your appearance transforms almost immediately. You will begin to not look

Embracing the New You

at life through rose colored glasses and start to see things for how they truly are.

Focusing more on yourself and your goals, needs and wants will help you to make sure you're building that platform you want. No longer will you be blind to your true self and hide behind a falsified image. Your creativity, eagerness to be educated and accomplish the things you want out of life will not be difficult but as easy as saying I can.

Your sense of presence will change. When you enter a room people will notice you. Your confidence will supersede the old you.

You won't just wear the confidence you'll be the confidence. Look I like to let people know you can wear Gucci but you should have the Gucci confidence to match. If you're caught wearing it but not being able to back it up with confidence than one or two things is true. One it's a fake and the second: it's borrowed.

If you're looking to be successful in life you must embrace the new you and be confident in who you are and what you want. Confidence is the key of creating your outside appearance.

Platform

Process of Embracing the New You: Step 10

1. See the change in yourself.

2. Accept the changes you are making in your life. The new thoughts and reactions you are bringing forth.

3. Every time you are confronted with a negative thought or action bring forth the new you.

4. Practice the new you often.

5. Repeat these steps whenever needed.

CHAPTER 11

Turn Your Fears into Accomplishments

Fear! Just the mention of the word brings people to peak at the next few words slowly on the page. Why? Well its part of the unknown. Having a sense of fear is something that is brought on by the mind. When you have the fear of failing that is nothing but something you yourself have conjured up in your conscious and subconscious mind.

"When we let our fears consume us and fester we stop ourselves from achieving and accomplishing our life long goals."

Platform

Mostly fear is just part of our imagination it's caused by an unpleasant emotion that makes us think something will do us harm, inflict unbearable pain or just out right threaten us. Not only do we become afraid of our fears but we hide from them and stay as far away from them as possible.

This is why we need to practice seeing our fear as an opportunity that has yet to be approached and start turning our fears into accomplishments. The new person you have come to be will not let you conjure up anymore fear. Why? You shouldn't have to ask why. But if you must know it's because you are confident in yourself to know that fear does not exist but only in the mind and that you created it. Think about it if you created it you can destroy it.

We create fear and it becomes an instant barrier. It sits there like a brick wall in front of our goals. This fear causes us to become afraid, ashamed and unresponsive to our goals that are screaming to be turned into accomplishments.

As we go through life letting fear consume us we create a long lasting battle with our internal self-awareness. We begin to settle and watch as we sink deeper into misery. Usually we sink so deep that it's hard to pull ourselves out or convince ourselves to try something again.

Think of a person that loves the water but cannot swim. They get in on the shallow side of the pool with their flotation device. They snuggle into the floating lounge chair with a few snacks and a drink to relax. Suddenly they drift off to sleep only to awaken hours later and find that they have floated over to the deep end.

Quickly they begin to panic and fear sets in. Looking for someone to assist them but no one is there, they try and

Turn Your Fears into Accomplishments

yell for help but no one comes. Too afraid to jump over the side and make a go for it they sit there.

Sitting there they being to just sulk but now they need to use the restroom and using the pool is not an option, embarrassment rears its ugly head. So they finally start to think.

They notice that the deep end is only 5 ft and they are 5'5inches. Knowing that they are in a position of control because they are taller than the threatening water they fear so much they jump in without a problem.

See when we calm down and think things through our fear becomes nothing but a minor obstacle standing in our way. The obstacle is so minute we are able to jump over it with relative easy. Finding out that we possess some type of control over our situations and possible outcomes helps us to move forward.

When we are put into fearful situations our rational side of the brain seems to be inoperative for a moment until we gain our composure. Most of us shut down until we are faced with not one but two obstacle at one time. In this persons case the second obstacle was embarrassment. Being that fear now has the state of embarrassment staring it in the face the person is confronted with making a choice.

Deciding to overcome our fear we find that we are placed in the mist of dealing with a few options. We quickly envision the different outcomes of our dilemma. Our outcomes usually start with negative thoughts of defeat and that stirs our fear and moves us further from accomplishing the tasks even more. These are the first things we need to change.

Platform

As we begin to face our fear we need to focus on positive outcomes. We need to create positive scenarios for every negative thought our fear tries to dig out of our subconscious.

First chose what the task is you're trying to accomplish. Start with something small.

Let's just say you have a fear of public speaking don't worry you are not alone. Just about an estimated 70 percent of people have this fear.

To break the ice with your fear envision your outcomes and make sure to have a positive scenario for every negative thought. After you've envisioned every conclusion now think about ways you can overcome those negative thoughts. How about taking a public speaking course? This helps the best of the best people get ready to address a small or large crowd. They offer great techniques that you can use when faced with a bout of doubt and fear.

Turn Your Fears into Accomplishments

Process of Turn Your Fears into Accomplishments: Step 11

1. First chose what the task is you're trying to accomplish. Start with something small.

CHAPTER 12

Put Your Plans into Action

When setting out to accomplish your goals you must set up a plan of action. Converting your fears into a plan of action is the first concrete step of heading toward your accomplishments. Creating a plan lets your mind know you are serious about getting rid of the unwanted host called fear.

"Letting go of our fear sets the mind free allowing it to unleash the sense of invincibility."

Without establishing a plan of action you are going to fail. You must put together a plan of attack in order to see your strengths and weaknesses.

Platform

In order to conquer the fear you must take action to destroy it. That may mean having to take classes or acting out your scenario by yourself or with friend's. Heck use stuffed animals or props if need be. Have fun with destroying your fear. Talk to yourself in the mirror that also helps. Once you can confront yourself face to face you will not feel as foolish and talking to someone else will seem like a breeze. You will most likely have the feeling you've done this before when talking to someone else.

The Plan of action should consist of answering a few questions.
1. What am I afraid of?
2. Why am I afraid of it?
3. How can I change my fear into an accomplishment?
4. When am I going to change it?
5. Where will this all happen?

For the first question "What am I afraid of", you must look deep within yourself and be honest. Finding the exact reason of what you are afraid of is important to defeating your fear. Not being honest with yourself as to what the fear really is will give you poor results. So use *honesty* at all times when devising a plan of action.

Next you need to dig deep and figure out what made you so afraid to confront this issue. You may come to find out it is something silly or from your childhood. Maybe your fear steams from self-doubt because of being teased as a child. Believe me we've all been there but you must push pass this and recognize it as the thing that's holding you back from your goals.

Put Your Plans into Action

Now is the time for you to put your thinking cap on tight. Once you've figure out what the fear is and why you are so afraid of it you need to put into action a plan of how to overcome it. How can you turn what has been a dark cloud over you for so long; into a bright and colorful rainbow a trophy for your life?

It may take some time and serious research to figure out the step you need to conquering your fear. Seeking professional knowledge, going back to school or finding out facts to support you through this moment is crucial.

If you are required to get some training, take a cooking class, step into the gym for the first time; muster up the courage to make new friends or getting the courage to face a negative person you need to figure out when and where this is going to happen. You can't forget to establish a when and where. Those two steps put your plan of action into motion. Set an actual date and a place where you will conquer your fear.

Whatever you do don't let your fear win by consuming you and preventing you from becoming the person you want to be.

Once you have finally conquered one goal move on to the next. Don't fret if you didn't do as well as you hoped to do because you can and will try again. The more you are persistent with tackling your fear you will wonder why you ever had the fear in the first place.

Platform

Try Again

Once you have faced your fear within its actual environment and if it hasn't gone well please don't think that you've failed. You must stand your ground and fight another day. Sometimes we try things and don't like it but realize if we had to do it again we could. That my dear is an accomplishment! When you feel this way you don't fear the task, you just rather not do it. Finding out what the goal or accomplishment means to you is key.

You must look for the victory in every task that you do. For every try there is an accomplishment of some sort. It's up to you to look for and recognize what you were able to do new this time and compare it to what you couldn't do before.

Throughout the journey of turning your fears into accomplishments you will find out something's can no longer be classified as a fear. Instead they just turn into things we don't like to do or can careless for. You just need to know no matter what you have made an accomplishment.

On the other hand if you are still having difficulty with conquering this mind induced feeling called fear and if it's about a goal or task you need to try again. You must keep trying and getting back on the bike after you've fallen off. This is the only way you're going to learn to ride. You can't ride with training wheels forever. If you do, you will go nowhere fast. So let yourself loose on your fear and keep trying until you've found your way.

Put Your Plans into Action

Put Your Plans into Action: Step 12

The Plan of action should consist of answering a few questions.

1. What am I afraid of?
2. Why am I afraid of it?
3. How can I change my fear into an accomplishment?
4. When am I going to change it?
5. Where will this all happen?

CHAPTER 13

Jump Take a Chance

Many times we are approached with opportunities and often we hesitate to take advantage of them. Sometimes these chances we are presented with in life are just unbelievable.

There are two types of opportunities we are faced with. First are the ones that make you feel like a stroke of luck has just rained down on you. Just like the feeling you get when you play monopoly and get to pass go and collect your two hundred bucks.

Then there are the unbelievable and rare opportunities. You know the once in a life time, this is too good to be true chances. When these rare opportunities show up and out of nowhere we tend to be in disbelief and our joy becomes tainted with dismay.

Platform

> "If one allows themselves to become stagnate with life. Rare chances become invisible and the eye of optimistic opportunity becomes faded."

Fear of things that are too good to be true puts a damper on our lives and prevents us from jumping and taking a chance. Instead of throwing caution to the wind we become filled with every thought of how it's not going to work.

Exceeding at anything in the real world requires taking drastic leaps of faith. The action must be preceded by the continuous thought of an "I can do it" attitude. With ever leap of faith one must have an established mindset that is fourth coming and positive.

Some think that taking leaps of faith without carefully calculating the outcome is downright ridiculous and plain irresponsible. Well I'm here to tell you not every chance or opportunity comes with the time to spare for you to do endless research.

Throwing caution to the wind and jumping at a chance is not being irresponsible if you don't have all the proper calculations in place. In fact most of the time your perceived notions about what the primary outcome will be is wrong.

I know that in earlier chapters I tell you that you have some control over outcomes and that is true but you don't have complete control. That's where flukes come into place. These flukes could be complications or rare opportunities that pop up.

Jump Take a Chance

Look things happen and sometimes where you thought you wanted to end up isn't the best place for you. Have you ever stopped for a moment and thought there can actually be another place for you.

Let's take this scenario into consideration. Say your job is looking to promote someone in your section to a new position. You look over the qualifications for the new position and your skills check every box down to the tee. After carefully debating if you are ready to take on such a large role you decided to submit your resume for consideration.

Just about a week has passed and your boss calls you into their office. Sitting there your mind races wondering if you have gotten the position and if not you're prepared to give a speech to tell your boss why they should choose you.

Suddenly your boss tells you after reviewing your resume it was decided that you would be the best person for the position. Filled with joy and excitement you sit at the edge of your seat. Your boss then tells you that an unexpected position has become available and you have been recommended for it. Shocked and astounded that your boss is telling you that the company is losing a head of the department due to retirement and they have recommended you to fill the executive position, you sit there.

After about five minutes your boss says the position is yours if you want it but you must give an answer now.

See it's these rare moments in life that can alter everything about our outcome. We have the option to follow our previous vision but sometimes there is a bigger plan setup for us. Not all the time will you be given the chance to think if something is or isn't right for you. At

Platform

some point throwing caution to the wind and going on a hunch at an unbelievable opportunity is something you must do.

There are only a few things to do and few questions to consider before making your decision. Being that you have a fraction of a few moments to make the decision you must consider a few things and this is only if you have a spouse and children.

If you have a spouse, excuse yourself from the room for a moment that's if you can and call your spouse immediately. In some cases this may not be wise or permitted so you must make the best judgment you can. Personal note this is your life and you must live with your choices regardless of what others think or feel.

Next would be to consider if this is for you and are you ready to sacrifice and alter your life immediately for this position. You will always have a few questions to ask yourself before you jump off the cliff and that is fine but don't forget to JUMP!

Jump Take a Chance

Process of Jump Take a Chance: Step 13

1. Is this something I really want to take on?
2. Am I willing to change today for this?
3. It's now or never am I ready?
4. Now Jump!

CHAPTER 14

Don't Settle

Throughout this journey you have transformed yourself into an new person. You have enhanced the true essences of yourself and you are ready for the world to see you. You've faced your negativity head on. Demolished old ways of thinking and put to rest those that bring you and your world down.

The steps that you've taken have proven to be the most memorable ones you have achieved so far. Please remember you have more memorable moments coming and a portfolio to keep developing of your life accomplishments. As you continue to perfect the new you, you must remember to never settle.

Platform

"When we let ourselves settle into defeat or glory we destroy ourselves and all the hard work we've put fourth toward our growth."

Take notice of your actions between long breaks of taking on your unachieved goals. If you notice that it's been more than a month since you've set out to learn something new or tackle a long awaited goal, try to find your motivation. Try and initiate a positive movement toward starting and taking on your next challenge.

Sometimes that next challenge can seem to be a bigger obstacle than we thought. Maybe looking at it you feel some type of resistance that's keeping you from tackling it. Well the best thing for you to do is head steadfast into it and don't think about the difficulty of it. This way once you're actually in it you can take it one step at a time making sure not to overwhelm yourself by conjuring up things in your mind that may or may not ever occur.

Try to move quickly into your next adventure don't become comfortable in your new setting especially when you have a lot of things to accomplish. Believe me you will always have a new goal waiting for you as you finish one to the next. For every goal you accomplish and ever new encounter you have a new goal pops into the empty space you have on your list. So don't get to comfortable in thinking you've accomplished everything on your goal list. That's a list that goes on just as long as you do.

Becoming comfortable in life is nice but it starts to fade your platform away. Continue to challenge yourself no matter the outcome of your task. Don't stand there and

Don't Settle

settle for defeat and surely don't stand there and settle for your status in the mist of glory.

Keep the platform you have created growing. There are always more obstacles in life to tackle and settling at one victory will and can cause your platform to collapse. Maintain your platform by setting out to conquer and achieve your goals even if one at a time.

Stop to bask in the glory and embrace the feeling of victory but don't settle and stop there. Stay moving forward. Every day you spend breathing is another day to tackle something or learn something new.

Stay driven by what is passionate to you and make sure you know when it is natural, not forced. Keep your focus on the prize and remember to walk with humility. Confidence is the key to being successful and you must harbor this emotion.

In every task you decide to take on plant the seed of success in your mind. Envision the process of exceeding every obstacle that stands before you and in the way of obtaining your goal. Never once let the thought of failing or your past failure consume your existence and push you away from the task you've set out to conquer.

Platform

Process of Don't Settle: Step 14

1. When you have achieved or attempted to face your one goal move on to the next.

2. If you find yourself becoming comfortable and content with where you are in life make a quick analysis of the situation and head straight out to achieve your next goal.

3. Look over your list of goals repeatedly and as you cross some off new ones should take their place.

Thank You

To all that have taken the time out to read and support my book I would like to personally thank you. In your strides to find and embrace the new you I wish you good luck and a successful journey.

Feel free to share your thoughts with me and stay up to date with what I have coming to the forefront next; by joining my blog site at www.tiesbowtieslipstick.com (it's free).

Notes:

Notes:

Notes:

www.ingramcontent.com/pod-product-compliance
Lightning Source LLC
Chambersburg PA
CBHW070931160426
43193CB00011B/1651